EXPLORING COUNTRIES
Bolivia

by Lisa Owings

GLORIA

BELLWETHER MEDIA · MINNEAPOLIS, MN

Note to Librarians, Teachers, and Parents:

Blastoff! Readers are carefully developed by literacy experts and combine standards-based content with developmentally appropriate text.

Level 1 provides the most support through repetition of high-frequency words, light text, predictable sentence patterns, and strong visual support.

Level 2 offers early readers a bit more challenge through varied simple sentences, increased text load, and less repetition of high-frequency words.

Level 3 advances early-fluent readers toward fluency through increased text and concept load, less reliance on visuals, longer sentences, and more literary language.

Level 4 builds reading stamina by providing more text per page, increased use of punctuation, greater variation in sentence patterns, and increasingly challenging vocabulary.

Level 5 encourages children to move from "learning to read" to "reading to learn" by providing even more text, varied writing styles, and less familiar topics.

Whichever book is right for your reader, Blastoff! Readers are the perfect books to build confidence and encourage a love of reading that will last a lifetime!

This edition first published in 2015 by Bellwether Media, Inc.

No part of this publication may be reproduced in whole or in part without written permission of the publisher. For information regarding permission, write to Bellwether Media, Inc., Attention: Permissions Department, 5357 Penn Avenue South, Minneapolis, MN 55419.

Library of Congress Cataloging-in-Publication Data

Owings, Lisa.
 Bolivia / by Lisa Owings.
    pages cm. – (Blastoff! readers: Exploring Countries)
 Summary: "Developed by literacy experts for students in grades three through seven, this book introduces young readers to the geography and culture of Bolivia"– Provided by publisher.
 Audience: Ages 7-12.
 Includes bibliographical references and index.
 ISBN 978-1-60014-984-9 (hardcover : alkaline paper)
 1. Bolivia–Juvenile literature. I. Title.
 F3308.5.O95 2014
 984–dc23
                                                                    2014003682

Contents

Bolivia is nestled in the middle of South America. A fairly large country, it covers 424,164 square miles (1,098,581 square kilometers). Bolivia has two capital cities. The main capital, La Paz, lies in a **canyon** near the western border. Most of the government works in La Paz. However, the **Supreme Court** remains to the south in the historic capital of Sucre.

Bolivia is a **landlocked** country. It shares a long border with Brazil to the north and east. Argentina and Paraguay lie to the south and southeast. Across the Andes Mountains to the southwest is Chile. Bolivia shares Lake Titicaca with its western neighbor, Peru.

Peru

Pacific Ocean

N
W   E
S

Brazil

Lake
Titicaca

Bolivia

La Paz

Sucre

Paraguay

Chile

Argentina

Altiplano

Western Bolivia sits high in the Andes Mountains. The Cordillera Occidental range runs along the border with Chile. To the east are the sharper peaks of the Cordillera Oriental. Between the two ranges, the land flattens into the **barren** Altiplano, or "High **Plateau**." Large lakes and white **salt flats** are cradled within the Altiplano.

The ridges and deep **gorges** of the Yungas trace the northeastern edges of the Andes. Hills and **fertile** valleys southeast of the mountains offer gentler slopes. The rest of eastern Bolivia is a wide **plain** called the Oriente. Rivers move slowly across its forests, swamps, and grasslands. Many of these rivers will eventually join the Amazon.

fun fact

The mountains and Altiplano are cool year-round. Eastern Bolivia is almost always warm.

Yungas

Lake Titicaca is the second largest lake in South America. It lies partly in Peru and partly in Bolivia. Surrounded by mountains, it is one of the highest lakes on Earth. Its waters give life to the dry Altiplano. Catfish and trout swim beneath the lake's surface. Titicaca is also a gathering place for water birds. Even flamingos flock to its shores.

Lake Titicaca contains around 40 islands. Some were home to **native** peoples before Europeans arrived. **Ruins** on the islands and lakeshores show how some of these peoples lived long ago. Many Bolivians still rely on Lake Titicaca for their way of life.

fun fact

The Uru people live on human-made "islands" of floating reeds in the middle of the lake. Each island holds several woven huts. The boats the Uru use are also made of reeds.

Did you know?

Lake Titicaca is the highest lake in the world on which large ships can freely travel.

llamas

Bolivia's wildlife is as **diverse** as its landscape. Llamas and alpacas live high in the mountains with their rarer cousins, guanacos and vicuñas. Woolly fur keeps these animals warm. Spectacled bears stay out of sight in misty mountain forests. Huge Andean condors wheel overhead. These **scavengers** are the largest flying birds in South America.

river dolphin

capybaras

rhea

! fun fact

Giant ostrich-like birds called rheas bound across Bolivia's grasslands. At around 50 pounds (23 kilograms) each, they are too heavy to fly.

The plains are home to armadillos and giant anteaters. Capybaras, the world's largest rodents, also roam there. In the forests lurk spotted jaguars. Pig-like tapirs are careful to avoid these big cats. Monkeys and sloths keep watch from the trees, where toucans and parrots also **roost**. Pink river dolphins play in the country's streams.

! fun fact

You can often tell where Bolivian women are from by the hats they wear. High-topped bowler hats are popular in La Paz. In Sucre and Cochabamba, wide-brimmed hats top heads.

More than 10 million people live in Bolivia. About six out of every ten are native to the area. The largest native groups are the Quechua and Aymara. Their languages are official in Bolivia.

A few Bolivians have **ancestors** from Spain and other European countries. Some early Europeans and natives raised families together. The children of these mixed families are called *mestizos*. Today, about three out of every ten Bolivians are *mestizos*. Most Europeans and *mestizos* speak Spanish, another official language. Spanish is the most widely spoken language in Bolivia.

Speak Spanish!

English	Spanish	How to say it
hello	hola	OH-lah
good-bye	adiós	ah-dee-OHS
yes	sí	SEE
no	no	NOH
please	por favor	POHR fah-VOR
thank you	gracias	GRAH-see-uhs
friend (male)	amigo	ah-MEE-goh
friend (female)	amiga	ah-MEE-gah

Most Bolivians live in cities. Wealthy families live in large homes or modern apartments. Poorer families build small homes on the outskirts of the city. Instead of buying cars, most people use buses and taxis to get around. City shops and restaurants stay open late into the night on the plains. In mountain cities, the chilly night air encourages people to head home early.

In the countryside, homes are often made of **adobe** and topped with straw roofs. Children help their parents with farm work and household chores. They walk or ride their bikes to get to school. Bolivians in the countryside buy and sell their goods at open-air markets.

Where People Live in Bolivia

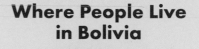

countryside
33%

cities
67%

Bolivian children start school at age 6. They learn to read and write in Spanish and their native language. Many children have to leave school before age 13. Their families need help on the farm or cannot afford school supplies. For children in the countryside, it is often also hard to get to school.

About one out of every four Bolivians attends secondary school. Those who complete four years of secondary school can apply to college. They have to pass an exam to attend one of the country's universities. Most college students graduate after five years and are ready to go to work.

Where People Work in Bolivia

farming 32%

manufacturing 20%

services 48%

fun fact

Llamas and alpacas are important to workers in the mountains. These animals can carry heavy loads. They are also valued for their soft, warm wool.

Bolivia is rich in **natural resources**. Many Bolivians work to harvest them from the earth. They mine tin, silver, and gold. They also dig for oil and natural gas. Farmers grow soybeans, coffee beans, and cotton in the valleys and lowlands. Potatoes are grown in the mountains. Bolivia's forests produce valuable wood and Brazil nuts.

Factory workers turn the country's resources into fuels, food products, and clothing. About half of Bolivians have **service jobs**. Those who work in restaurants and hotels mainly serve **tourists**. Others work in banks, schools, and shops. Many Bolivians run their own small businesses.

Bolivians have a passion for *fútbol*, or soccer. Children make soccer balls out of shopping bags or other found materials. They gather for games after school and on weekends. People also love to watch the pros play at soccer stadiums. Golfers enjoy stunning views while playing on courses in the Andes. Other popular sports include volleyball and bicycle racing.

Young Bolivians like to watch television, play video games, and visit Internet cafés. Movie theaters in large cities draw crowds. Friends often meet to chat over a cup of tea. Throughout Bolivia, local festivals offer singing, dancing, and other **traditions** for young and old.

fun fact

Spinning tops is a favorite game for Bolivian children. Skilled spinners can pick up their tops and keep them spinning in their hands!

Did you know?

Andean potatoes are often left outside for several cold nights and sunny days until they dry out. Then they can be stored for a long time.

Food in the Andes is **hearty** and spicy. Most dishes include potatoes along with chicken, fish, or other meats. Everything is flavored with a spicy sauce called *llajua*. Warming stews and soups are also common in the mountains. *Sopa de mani* is a soup flavored with meat, vegetables, and peanuts.

Fruits and vegetables are more plentiful in the valleys and lowlands. Beef is the most common meat there. Bolivians love to eat it fresh off the grill. In cities, *salteñas* are a filling morning snack. These handheld pies are stuffed with meat, vegetables, and spicy sauce. In the afternoon, Bolivians head to the nearest tea house for a hot drink and a sweet pastry.

fun fact

Pique a lo macho is one of Bolivia's most popular dishes. Beef, sausages, boiled eggs, and vegetables are served in a mound over fried potatoes.

pique a lo macho

salteñas

Did you know?
Bolivia celebrates its independence from Spain on August 6.

Carnaval

Carnaval is one of the biggest holidays in Bolivia. Thousands crowd the city of Oruro in February or March. The music, dancing, and colorful parades go on for days. During the following weeks of **Lent**, the mood becomes more serious. Religious Bolivians attend church during the week of Easter.

In June, Aymara gather for *Inti Raymi*. They celebrate the winter sun with ancient **rituals**. This festival also marks the beginning of the Aymara New Year. The Fiesta de San Roque takes place in August or September in Tarija. It honors the city's **patron saint**, who is also the patron saint of dogs. People watch a large procession and dress their dogs in ribbons.

fun fact

The *Alasitas* festival in January honors Ekeko, the god of good luck. Markets sell miniature houses, cars, and other items. People attach miniatures of the items they want to statues of Ekeko.

Did you know?

Tiwanaku farmers dug channels for water between their crop beds. The water held the sun's heat and kept the crops from freezing at night.

Long ago, Tiwanaku was the seat of one of the greatest **civilizations** in South America. It started as a small village near Lake Titicaca. The people who lived there were skilled farmers. By 500 CE, Tiwanaku had grown into a great city. Its people ruled parts of modern-day Bolivia, Argentina, Chile, and Peru for centuries. In the 1100s, Tiwanaku's power faded.

Gate of the Sun

Bolivians are still uncovering the secrets of Tiwanaku. Its ruins are all that remain of this mysterious civilization. A stepped pyramid marks the holiest place in the city. The ruins of a large temple contain a beautifully carved stone doorway. This "Gate of the Sun" may once have served as a calendar. Today it provides a window into Bolivia's ancient past.

Fast Facts About Bolivia

Bolivia's Flag

Bolivia's flag has horizontal strips of red, yellow, and green. The red stands for bravery. The yellow represents the land's natural resources. The green symbolizes Bolivia's fertile farmland. The government flag includes a coat of arms in the center. This flag was adopted in 1888.

Official Name: Plurinational State of Bolivia

Area: 424,164 square miles (1,098,581 square kilometers); Bolivia is the 28th largest country in the world.

Capital Cities:	La Paz (administrative), Sucre (constitutional)
Important Cities:	Santa Cruz, Cochabamba, Oruro, Tarija
Population:	10,461,053 (July 2013)
Official Languages:	Spanish, Quechua, Aymara
National Holiday:	Independence Day (August 6)
Religions:	Christian (97%), other/none (3%)
Major Industries:	mining, farming, manufacturing, services, tourism
Natural Resources:	tin, zinc, silver, gold, oil, timber, natural gas
Manufactured Products:	fuels, food products, clothing, paper products
Farm Products:	soybeans, coffee beans, cotton, corn, rice, potatoes, Brazil nuts
Unit of Money:	Boliviano; the Boliviano is divided into 100 centavos.

Glossary

adobe—bricks made of clay and straw that are dried in the sun

ancestors—relatives who lived long ago

barren—having very few plants

canyon—a narrow river valley with steep, tall sides

civilizations—highly developed, organized communities

diverse—made up of many different types or coming from many different backgrounds

fertile—able to support growth

gorges—deep, narrow valleys with steep, rocky sides

hearty—filling and satisfying

landlocked—completely surrounded by land

Lent—the forty weekdays before the Christian holiday of Easter

native—originally from a specific place

natural resources—materials in the earth that are taken out and used to make products or fuel

patron saint—a saint who is believed to look after a country or group of people

plain—a large area of flat land

plateau—an area of flat, raised land

rituals—acts that are always performed in the same way, often as part of a religious ceremony

roost—to sleep or rest in trees

ruins—the physical remains of human-made structures

salt flats—flat areas where a body of saltwater has dried up and left a layer of salt

scavengers—animals that feed on dead or rotting flesh

service jobs—jobs that perform tasks for people or businesses

supreme court—the highest court in a country or state

tourists—people who travel to visit another place

traditions—customs, ideas, or beliefs handed down from one generation to the next

To Learn More

AT THE LIBRARY

DiPiazza, Francesca. *Bolivia in Pictures*. Minneapolis, Minn.: Twenty-First Century Books, 2008.

Gelletly, LeeAnne. *Bolivia*. Broomall, Penn.: Mason Crest Publishers, 2008.

Gorrell, Gena K. *In the Land of the Jaguar: South America and Its People*. Toronto, Ont.: Tundra Books, 2007.

ON THE WEB

Learning more about Bolivia is as easy as 1, 2, 3.

1. Go to www.factsurfer.com.

2. Enter "Bolivia" into the search box.

3. Click the "Surf" button and you will see a list of related web sites.

With factsurfer.com, finding more information is just a click away.

Index